P9-AOY-126

WATERFORD TOWNSHIP
PUBLIC LIBRARY

W9-CEL-178

DISCARD

U.S. Navy cruisers
J 623.825 RUS

Rustad, Martha E.
Waterford Township Library

DISCARD

MILITARY VEHICLES

U.S.
NAVY
CRUISERS

by Martha E. H. Rustad

Reading Consultant:
Barbara J. Fox
Reading Specialist
North Carolina State University

Capstone
press

Mankato, Minnesota

Blazers is published by Capstone Press,
151 Good Counsel Drive, P.O. Box 669, Mankato, Minnesota 56002.
www.capstonepress.com

Copyright © 2007 by Capstone Press. All rights reserved.
No part of this publication may be reproduced in whole or in part, or stored in a retrieval
system, or transmitted in any form or by any means, electronic, mechanical,
photocopying, recording, or otherwise, without written permission of the publisher.
For information regarding permission, write to Capstone Press,
151 Good Counsel Drive, P.O. Box 669, Dept. R, Mankato, Minnesota 56002.
Printed in the United States of America

Library of Congress Cataloging-in-Publication Data
Rustad, Martha E. H. (Martha Elizabeth Hillman), 1975–
    U.S. Navy cruisers / by Martha E. H. Rustad.
    p. cm.—(Blazers. Military vehicles)
    Summary: "Describes U.S. Navy cruisers, including their design, weapons,
equipment, crew, and missions"—Provided by publisher.
    Includes bibliographical references and index.
    ISBN-13: 978-0-7368-6459-6 (hardcover)
    ISBN-10: 0-7368-6459-8 (hardcover)
    1. Cruisers (Warships)—Juvenile literature. 2. Ticonderoga (Guided missile
cruiser)—Juvenile literature. I. Title. II. Series.
    V820.3.R88 2007
    623.825'30973—dc22   2006000519

Editorial Credits
Amber Bannerman, editor; Thomas Emery, set designer; Ted Williams, designer;
    Jo Miller, photo researcher/photo editor

Photo Credits
Check Six/George Hall, 28–29
DVIC, 12–13; Chuck Cavanaugh, 8–9; PH2 Robert Catalano, 4–5
Ted Carlson/Fotodynamics, 20–21
U.S. Navy Photo, 19 (bottom); IS1 Kenneth Moll, 27 (bottom); JOSN Matthew
    Olay, 25 (bottom); PHAN Konstandinos Goumenidis, 22–23; PHAN
    Patrick M. Bonafede, cover; PHC Todd Cichonowicz, 11 (top); PH1 Alan
    Warner, 11 (bottom); PH1 Brien Aho, 6–7; PH1 Michael W. Pendergrass,
    19 (top); PH1 Robert R. McRill, 25 (top), 26; PH2 Bob Houlihan, 16–17;
    PH2 Charles E. Hill, 19 (middle); PH2 Leland Comer, 14–15; PH3 David
    K. Simmons, 27 (top)

**Capstone Press thanks Rear Admiral Steven G. Smith, United States Navy
(Retired), for his assistance in preparing this book.**

1 2 3 4 5 6 11 10 09 08 07 06

TABLE OF CONTENTS

Cruisers 4

Design 8

Weapons and Equipment 14

Crew on a Mission. 22

Ticonderoga Class Cruiser Diagram 20

Glossary 30

Read More 31

Internet Sites 31

Index 32

CRUISERS

A warship cruises swiftly
ahead of its fleet. The cruiser
searches for enemy ships, aircraft,
and submarines.

OILER

CRUISER

AIRCRAFT CARRIER

DESTROYER

Some cruisers protect aircraft carriers and other ships. Other cruisers complete missions on their own.

DESTROYER

WATERFORD TOWNSHIP
PUBLIC LIBRARY

061730

DESIGN

The U.S. Navy currently uses cruisers from the Ticonderoga class. These cruisers have powerful weapons and sensors. They are built to move quickly.

Most cruisers are powered by four gas turbine engines. The engines turn two propellers that push the ship through the water.

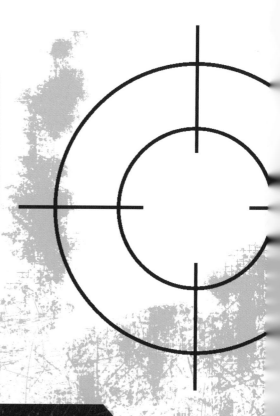

BLAZER FACT

The blades on a cruiser's propellers turn backward to stop the ship and to back it up.

PROPELLER

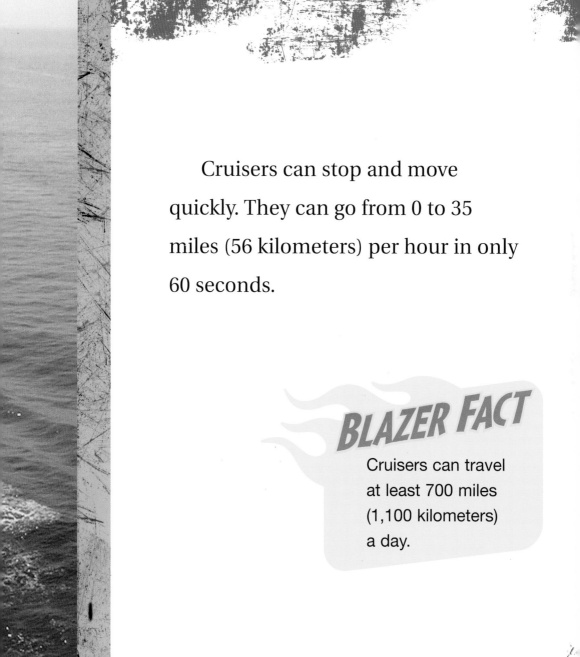

Cruisers can stop and move quickly. They can go from 0 to 35 miles (56 kilometers) per hour in only 60 seconds.

BLAZER FACT

Cruisers can travel at least 700 miles (1,100 kilometers) a day.

WEAPONS AND EQUIPMENT

A cruiser usually carries one or two helicopters. The helicopters search for enemies and protect the ship.

Cruisers find and track hundreds of possible targets with a radar system called Aegis. The Aegis system also guides missiles toward targets.

Cruiser weapons are always ready to fire. Vertical Launching Systems (VLS) store many kinds of missiles in their hatches. Missiles launch out of the hatches to destroy targets.

BLAZER FACT

Cruisers can attack targets anywhere. They can even fire on underwater targets like submarines.

HATCHES

VLS SYSTEM

MISSILE

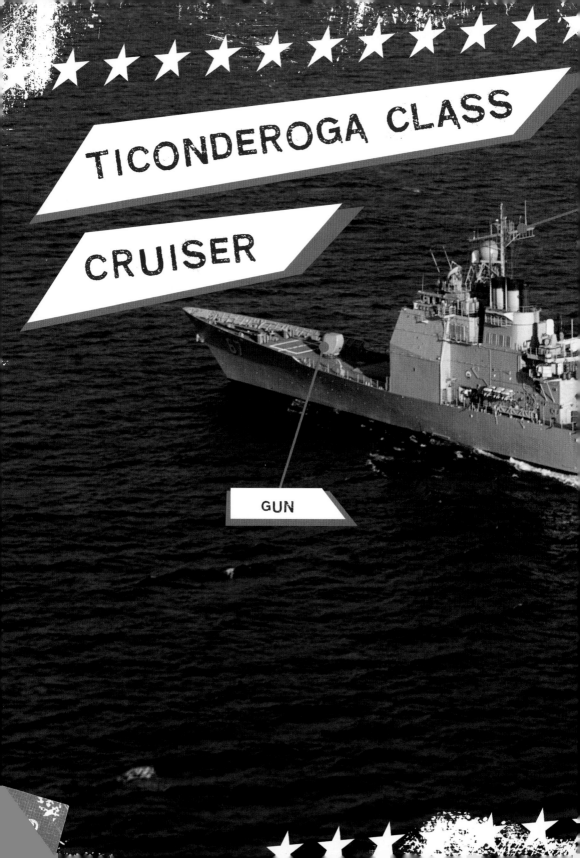

TICONDEROGA CLASS

CRUISER

GUN

RADIO
ANTENNAS

AEGIS RADAR

VLS SYSTEM

HELICOPTER
LANDING PAD

CREW ON A MISSION

More than 360 sailors live
and work on a Ticonderoga class
cruiser. Cruisers can refuel and get
more weapons and supplies at sea.

FUEL TUBE

Sailors do many jobs on cruisers. Some sailors check radar systems. Other sailors clean and maintain the ship.

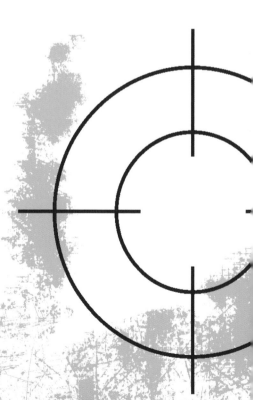

BLAZER FACT

Sailors on a cruiser work about 18 hours each day.

Cruisers are important parts
of U.S. Navy fleets. Cruisers find
and destroy enemies so they cannot
fire on other U.S. ships. Cruisers sail
the oceans to keep them safe for the
United States.

MANNING THE RAIL!

BLAZER FACT

When entering or leaving a port, the sailors dress in full uniform and stand near the rail of the ship. This is called manning the rail.

GLOSSARY

fleet (FLEET)—a group of warships under one command

hatch (HACH)—the part of the VLS system of a ship where missiles are stored and launch out of

missile (MISS-uhl)—an explosive weapon that can travel long distances

mission (MISH-uhn)—a military task

propeller (pruh-PEL-ur)—a set of rotating blades that push a ship through water

radar (RAY-dar)—equipment that uses radio waves to locate and guide objects

sensor (SEN-sur)—a device that can pick up and send signals

turbine engine (TUR-bine EN-juhn)—an engine powered by steam or gas; the steam or gas moves through the blades of a fanlike device and makes it turn.

READ MORE

Doeden, Matt. *The U.S. Navy*. The U.S. Armed Forces. Mankato, Minn.: Capstone Press, 2005.

Hamilton, John. *The Navy*. Defending the Nation. Edina, Minn.: Abdo, 2006.

Stone, Lynn M. *Cruisers*. Fighting Forces on the Sea. Vero Beach, Fla.: Rourke, 2006.

INTERNET SITES

FactHound offers a safe, fun way to find Internet sites related to this book. All of the sites on FactHound have been researched by our staff.

Here's how:
1. Visit *www.facthound.com*
2. Choose your grade level.
3. Type in this book ID **0736864598** for age-appropriate sites. You may also browse subjects by clicking on letters, or by clicking on pictures and words.
4. Click on the **Fetch It** button.
FactHound will fetch the best sites for you!

INDEX

Aegis, 17
aircraft, 4
aircraft carriers, 7

enemies, 4, 14, 26
engines, 10

fleets, 4, 26

hatches, 18
helicopters, 14

missions, 7

propellers, 10

radar, 17, 24

sailors, 22, 24, 29
sensors, 8
speed, 13
submarines, 4, 18

targets, 17, 18

Vertical Launching
    Systems (VLS), 18

weapons, 8, 18, 22
    missiles, 17, 18